Guide to a Happy, Healthy, and Successful Marriage

Danielle Pesch

ISBN 979-8-89243-875-9 (paperback)
ISBN 979-8-89243-876-6 (digital)

Christian Faith Publishing
832 Park Avenue
Meadville, PA 16335
www.christianfaithpublishing.com

Printed in the United States of America

To my baby brother, Joe, who went to be with Jesus in April
of 2022, who was so loving and so sweet. Even though he is
not here on earth with us anymore, he is still inspiring me
every day to live and to help others, like he always did.

To my amazing husband, Jason, who has always loved
me for all of me and always supported me. He has
given me the love and marriage to inspire this book
to help others. I love you so much, Jason!

To my loving brother, Josh, who has always been one of my best
friends and has taught me wisdom that I am so thankful for.

Lastly, but not least, to my mother, Christine, and grandfather
Danny for always loving me, praying for me, and teaching
me so much about love and wisdom. I would not be who
I am today without you two. I love you so much!

I also want to thank the Lord for putting the desire and
motivation in my heart to write this book to hopefully
help multiple people. All glory and praises to God!

CONTENTS

ADVICE ABOUT MARRIAGE FROM FAMILY AND FRIENDS

Before we dive in, I wanted to share advice from my friends and family that answers the following question: *What advice do you have for someone who is seeking a happy and successful marriage?*

You will notice a lot of responses are similar to topics in this book because good advice really does work if you really want to listen and apply it! If you have ever asked an old married couple that has been married for fifty-plus years how they lasted and have been together so long, you will hear similar responses as the ones below! No marriage is perfect. Marriage is hard, sacrificial, and hard work, but all of that is worth it and so rewarding.

I hope this is a blessing to you as much as hearing the responses were to me!

My advice would be to adjust expectations and to talk about them
before marriage and during constantly, also to communicate as
much as you can in the medium that makes it easier for you to
truly be honest and open and vulnerable with your other half. After
kids, it is super important to make the time and effort to connect,
even if it is just for a few minutes every day. Also, learn how to
love your spouse in *their* love language, and always keep the lines
of communication open for each other even when it is hard to do.

—Jaime Raifsnider

Forgiveness is necessary, as well as healthy boundaries put into place (this goes for extended family as well). We sometimes can forget that our spouses are human and are not perfect, so we can easily fall into unrealistic expectations. Holding grudges can kill intimacy. Forgiveness is key. Being able to consciously ground yourself in an argument and remembering your spouse is your teammate and not the enemy. It is us versus the problem at hand, not us against each other. Words hurt and cannot be taken back, so always speak respectfully and lovingly to your spouse. Privacy equals happiness. This means, your sister and whole family group text does not need to know that your spouse upset you for the tenth time this week. Inviting others into your private life is a recipe for disaster. You might have forgiven them, but your mom might not. Once you involve outsiders into your marriage, be prepared for unsolicited advice. A bad day does not mean a bad life. Marriage is hard; nobody has ever lied about that. The beautiful thing is, you can choose your hard. Choose your battles wisely, and always remember that if it were easy, it would not be worth the fight. Marriage is beautiful, messy, hard, selfless, and heart-wrenching but so worth it. It is definitely not for the weak.

—Stephanie Wall

Argue about the little stuff. Agree about the big stuff. Jim and I will get complaints about dishes that need to be done or about not saving the last bite, but when it comes to the big and hard stuff, we are on the same page. We talked a lot about kids, where we would want to live, when it was and was not okay to blow money. ("Is the mortgage paid?" for example.) We are good on that stuff.

—Alex McQueen

Communication is key. Never go to bed angry at one another!

—Julia Bosma

Praying together, having God a part of your relationship—God is top priority, then your spouse, then your kids, then everything else.

—Brittany Anne

You have to look at your relationship like you are a team, and you are both working together to accomplish things. You need good communication to keep things going long term. Always find time to do things together, even if it is just watching TV together weekly. Do a date night at least once monthly. You need to put your relationship over your kids sometimes. You and your partner are in this for life, and your kids will start their own lives at some point. Always be willing to work on your relationship. Marriage can be so tough, but when you find your soulmate, it is worth it.

—Sarah Boyle

Marriage is supposed to sanctify you. It is not about you/ your spouse's happiness (although that is not unimportant); it is a picture of Christ and the church. Once you lose sight of serving each other, the whole thing falls apart very quickly.

—Pamela Vande Polder

Marry someone you love living life with! We always say, "I love living life with you!" while we are eating dinner, driving, folding laundry, lying on the couch, grocery shopping, playing music, whatever! Have fun, and be silly!

—Jen Pesch-Ewers

I have always thought a date night is necessary (and to make it feel like it is your first date); secondly, for some, meeting with a counselor early on. It is a way to catch the little things before they become much bigger, uncontrollable things. It is a very wise counsel!

—Jim Brenneman

Each person in the marriage need only do one thing: Always do everything in your power to make your spouse as happy as possible to the best of your ability. Love is giving them everything you have to give unconditionally.

—Kenneth Croyle

The one thing I try to remember, no matter what, is this: Just be a nice human. It seems like people who get married forget that their spouse has a whole range of feelings and emotions too, so the conversations you have with them matter, but so does the way you have those conversations. Remember to be gentle and loving, even when you are upset. It goes such a long way in healing an argument.

—Kennedy Keck

God's agape love demonstrated by Jesus. Love is an action word, it is something we do and real action is the only way to communicate love to someone. Love comes entrenched in the laying down of one's own life because there is no room for selfishness in true love. It is an action that shows the other person you are willing to sacrifice your own self for their good.

—Grandpa (Danny) Green

Pray together, worship together, go to church together, honor each other, walk in love with each other, prefer the other above yourself, serve each other, encourage each other, date each other, romance each other, kiss each other, hold hands with each other.

—Christine Hirsch (Mom)

"Be devoted to one another in love. Honor one another above yourselves" (Romans 12:10). Love each other unconditionally and intentionally. Keep the Lord at the center of your marriage and family.

—Maria Hong

Romans 12:10: "Be devoted to one another in love. Honor one another above yourselves." Pray together daily. Serve God and each other.

—Brenda Haan

Marriage is not fifty-fifty. Each day, you wake up and give 100/100 to your marriage because only giving half of yourselves will keep you from being the best you can be.

—Chris Rousch

Marry your best friend, and know you are theirs. You can get through anything with your best friend by your side. Every relationship argues. It's a form of communication. Argue to understand and resolve, not to be mean. If you marry the person you can argue with and breathe that sigh of relief after, knowing that you both get it, that's it. You can't go through life not understanding how the other person feels, you won't get anywhere. The only other way to communicate this is to understand their love language. Do your best to be their best friend in the way they need. It's about both of you, don't be selfish. Love is everything but that.

—Blake Gulewicz

Marriage isn't fifty-fifty. Together you make up 100 percent. Some days one of you will struggle and only have 20 percent to give. Suck it up and pick up the extra 80 percent because they need you to.

—Brittany Brown

Respect and consideration are important for each other. You love each other, right? One should never think it is okay to overpower the other. No happiness will come from this. Have laughs as much as possible! As far as children, parents should show respect by not involving kids in their disagreements. Respect each other for the children's sake. Be a good example.

—Donna Thomas

My husband is a jokester and has the best sense of humor.
I hope this gives you a good laugh. I wanted his input so I asked him, "If your son came to you and asked you what a good marriage looks like, what would you tell him?"
His response was, "Happy wife, happy life." (He knows I dislike and disagree with this saying, so he said it on purpose to be funny.)
Me: "That is not good advice because your happiness matters too."
Him: "But when you are happy, I am happy too."
Me, blushing: "I love you. Is there anything else you would add as a quote?"
Him knowing I love happy meals: "Happy meals keep the happy feels."
His real advice is below.
"Really listen to your wife and give her your everything. Love is what you do. Love your wife, respect your wife, and make sure to spend quality time with her! Communication is everything. Make the effort to learn each other's love language."

—Jason Pesch

How I Went from Wanting Marriage to Not Ever Wanting to Get Married, to Changing My Perspective and Wanting Marriage Again

I remember being as young as twelve, and I could not wait to grow up to get married and be a wife. I remember wanting a husband who would be my best friend to do everything together, travel, and to love each other so much, just like romance movies.

Like any young person, I had hopes, dreams, goals, and had such a positive outlook on life and love, but I was also easily influenced and vulnerable. Eventually, growing up and being on your own is not as fun as I thought it seemed. Life happens to everyone, and you go through ups and downs, and your perspective changes. Your heart goes through tough times. You experience the cruelty of the real world. You are trying to figure out who you are, wanting to fit in and be liked.

For me being raised with faith, I strayed from the faith and decided to go along with the world's ways, which led to destruction, heartbreak, and being extremely deceived by what love even meant. I watched way too many movies and TV shows, listened to music that all depicted a warped, deceiving view of what love looks like. I hung out with the wrong crowds. I thought being controlled or someone being jealous meant they really loved me. I thought yelling was normal. I saw normalization of affairs and cheating. I thought my looks mattered so much that it was the only way people would love me. I thought that I had to be someone I was not to even find love. After a confusing, downward spiral of events, I concluded that I wanted nothing to do with love or marriage because I felt so bitter toward it. I let my heart grow cold. Sound familiar?

I realize now that my experiences, all that music I listened to, all of the movies and TV shows I watched really changed how I viewed reality, and it was a false sense of reality. After falling for the deception of what love was in the movies, I started to realize who I was becoming is not who I wanted to be nor who I was meant to be. I realized, being genuine, selfless, kind, honest, and humble, like I was before I was on my own, is what people do need and appreciate.

Growing through pain and adversity helps you to become a man or woman of character so you can become stronger from the adversities. Life is a learning and growing experience for all of us. Nobody is perfect. Our hearts deceive us, especially when we make decisions based on feelings or temporary emotions. It is so important, in any relationship we have but especially in marriage, that we learn grace and understanding for one another so that we can help each other grow and learn from our mistakes. Proverbs 4:23 says, "Above all else, guard your heart, for everything you do flows from it." How do we guide our heart? We must guide our eyes, ears, and thoughts because what we allow in flows out through our words and actions. The ways of this world will taint marriage, your marriage. Do not be deceived by the world. This means be careful what you watch, be careful what and who you listen to. If something produces bad fruit or negative emotions/thoughts, it will lead to a path of destruction. Guard your heart so you can help your spouse guard theirs!

I do not claim to be perfect or to know everything because I don't, and I am far from perfect. The reason my husband and I have such a healthy, blessed marriage is because we are two people who learned everything the hard way (strange that is how humans work, right?). Know we are not perfect nor ever will be. We have grace and forgiveness toward one another. Ephesians 4:32 says, "Be kind and compassionate to one another, forgiving each other, just as Christ our God forgave you." When we say we are sorry, we mean it, and we change to work on ourselves. We care about how we make each other feel and put each other's needs above our own. The world teaches you to do what makes you happy, to follow your heart, and just focus on yourself. I disagree with all of those. While happiness is important, happiness is not possible all of the time because life is full of ups and downs. (So is marriage.) To follow your heart means to follow your feelings and emotions, but emotions are fleeting and can cause us to act in a way we normally would not in our right mind or in a calm state of emotion. I disagree with just focusing on yourself because our entire purpose in life is to be here for and to help one another.

Marriage reflects our relationship with Jesus. Just like coming to Jesus requires surrender and dying to self, marriage also requires surrender. From the moment you say "I do," you are surrendering yourself to your spouse. Life is not about you anymore; it is about your spouse. While our own needs and happiness are important, your needs and happiness come second in marriage. Whoever said marriage is not easy is telling the truth because it is not easy. It is sacrificial and about serving your spouse. When you serve each other, put each other's needs above your own, your marriage will succeed. It does not feel like work to us. We genuinely enjoy making each other happy, helping each other out, doing acts of service for each other, and just spending life together. I pray and hope for this kind of marriage for everyone! The success of your marriage all depends on the amount of work, effort, wisdom you acquire, and appreciation you provide. It starts with you learning self-discipline. Remember, marriage is selfless, not selfish. When you start serving your spouse, you will see the result and impact it has on your marriage. They are more likely to want to serve you back, you will be filled with joy, and you will watch your marriage flourish!

When my husband came into my life, I was not looking for a relationship. My mindset was, *I am never dating anyone again. I am staying single forever.* I was still distancing myself from God at this point, but God was not distancing himself from me. I was working as a server at the time, and he was a part of a softball league that would come into my work. One day, he came in alone, and I heard that voice in me, asking him to have a drink with me. I am not the type of person to "make a move," as they say it, or confront anyone, but I did. Then after that first night of hanging out and talking, God spoke to me and said, "That's going to be your husband one day." Because of the place I was at in my life, I naturally questioned it and said to myself, "What? Am I going crazy?" I never told him that until we got married because my thinking was, *I think I am crazy, so he will think I am crazy*, which is all funny now, and we understand it now.

My husband changed my life and helped me view life and love in a positive way again. He showed such honesty, humility, respect, patience, understanding, and hope, which ultimately brought me back to God again, and I am so thankful. I had changed my mind about wanting marriage about six months into our new relationship but never mentioned it until about two years in. We were both on the same page when we first met as far as a big no to marriage. We helped change each other's minds, perspectives, and most of all our hearts toward it, which of course God gets all the credit for doing that work in us. I always knew it takes about three to five years to truly know someone. That was the time frame I told myself I would wait before I got engaged or married to someone. We were engaged a little after three years of being together and married a month after our fifth anniversary. We have been together just over six years, and we love each other more and more each day. How is that, you ask? The world has normalized and almost glorified divorce and breaking up (giving up on each other when things go bad), but that is because there is no guidance to help us all be the spouse and person we need to be or how to work through problems. Our perspectives on people, life, marriage have been completely programmed and socially engineered over time to think negatively and focus on the negative, rather than positively and lovingly. Just like in the faith, when trials are met, it can cause people to lose faith and fall away from the faith and blame God. In marriage, when trials come, the world does not train us how to overcome the trials, work through them, or see them as a lesson to learn, grow, or to improve ourselves. The world teaches us there is something wrong with the relationship and to just give up, leave, find someone better/new. When we should be learning how to let God make ourselves new and better while learning how to properly love and know our spouses in order to work through issues maturely with love and grace for one another. To be clear, I know there are circumstances when divorce/leaving is absolutely warranted, and those circumstances are not what I am referring to.

Before we got married, we met with my grandfather, who officiated our wedding to go over the ceremony. He is a very wise man of God, who has taught us so much. He asked us why we were getting married and what our definition of love was. He explained that love is not just a feeling; it is an action word. Love is what we do. We choose to love, and we show love in our actions each day. This statement is true, and love is really a choice we make each day. We choose to serve each other, to love each other past the flaws, and to honor each other even on the hard days. The Bible verse 1 Corinthians 13 explains what love is and what love is not and how we are nothing without having love, to love even when it is hard to. Verses 4 through 7 are often heard in weddings. But this chapter is alive, and if you really apply it to marriage, you are set up for a successful and lasting marriage. My advice is to seek the wisdom of God and not the wisdom of this world. The wisdom I have received is not of this world and has never failed me. The wisdom of this world can really set you up for destruction and failure as I have learned firsthand from my entire (so far thirty years) life experience.

We live in a relativistic world, where what is acceptable and what is not is always changing. God's word and promises remain the same. The world will create standards of marriage and relationships to fit its own agendas and opinions. The truth of God's word never changes, and God remains the same yesterday, today, and always, which is such an encouragement in marriage.

> If I speak in the tongues of men and of
> angels, but have not love, I am a noisy gong or a
> clanging cymbal. And if I have prophetic powers,
> and understand all mysteries and all knowledge,

and if I have all faith, so as to remove mountains, but have not love, I am nothing. If I give away all I have, and if I deliver up my body to be burned, but have not love, I gain nothing.

Love is patient and kind; love does not envy or boast; it is not arrogant or rude. It does not insist on its own way; it is not irritable or resentful; it does not rejoice at wrongdoing, but rejoices with the truth. Love bears all things, believes all things, hopes all things, endures all things.

Love never ends. As for prophecies, they will pass away; as for tongues, they will cease; as for knowledge, it will pass away. For we know in part and we prophesy in part, but when the perfect comes, the partial will pass away. When I was a child, I spoke like a child, I thought like a child, I reasoned like a child. When I became a man, I gave up childish ways. For now we see in a mirror dimly, but then face to face. Now I know in part; then I shall know fully, even as I have been fully known.

So now faith, hope, and love abide, these three; but the greatest of these is love. (1 Corinthians 13)

Though man wrote the chapters of the Bible, it is important to understand and remember that the words came from God. The writer of Corinthians, the apostle Paul, is explaining that anything done without love is meaningless to God. You can have all of the spiritual gifts, wisdom, or faith in the world, but if you do not have love, it is meaningless. As followers of Christ, we are called to use the gifts God gave us to imitate Jesus's love by focusing not on ourselves but others' good. Our gifts do not impress God but using them with the same love as Jesus does. This entire verse is God's way of showing, if we live for the Lord and obey with the action love according to God's commands and putting others first and serving them.

If you are someone who has given up the idea of love or marriage, do me a favor and cling to even a grain of sand–sized piece of hope. While I had thought I lost all hope, I secretly, deep down, clung to a tiny grain of hope inside. If you are reading this book, you likely are my friend or family supporting my first book (totally kidding), or in all seriousness, you are someone who is serious about wanting to have a happy, successful, and healthy marriage. Whether you are married right now or wanting to get married, I pray this blesses and helps at least one person!

CHAPTER 1

Learning Each Other

Once you meet someone and first start dating, you spend the first few months really getting to know each other: what your interests are, what you like to do, who they are, and so on. However, getting to know each other does not stop after a few months. For as long as you are together, especially when you are married, you are constantly still learning about each other. As we grow older, we grow wiser and change, so we are constantly learning and loving each new version of our spouse as the years go by, which is exciting and fun, if you make it that way!

On one of our first nights of really talking and getting to know each other, I grew a respect for my husband that I never had experienced with anyone before. He opened up to me about his past, was so honest about who he was and who he was on the path to being. This resulted in me doing the same as I felt safe with him after only talking to him two or three times at this point. What I realized was that we were two people who made multiple mistakes in the past, were self-aware of our own flaws, and at the same point in our lives, trying to move forward and become better than we were before. We were both turning around and going in the opposite direction as we were before. We were humbled by our pasts, learned from our pasts, and I think that really sparked our relationship instantly as we became an instant couple from there.

Being human, we naturally want to be able to be ourselves openly around one another and be accepted for that. But then, we experience heartache, someone being mean to us that affects our confidence/self-esteem, or life-changing situations that change us and may make us pull back on being ourselves. As a result, we build walls, are scared to let anyone in, or even don't allow ourselves to be vulnerable in order to protect ourselves.

One of the biggest lies the world tells us is, we have to hide who we are or who we were, especially if it is shameful or embarrassing. The world does shame us or make us feel bad for making mistakes. In fact, sometimes it seems like the world wants us to fail. The world tends to write people off when they make mistakes or there is a conflict, instead of learning to understand or working the conflict out. This is what causes so many issues in relationships and marriages in hiding the flaws and the mistakes, when really, we are meant to be open, honest, and empathetic with each other so we can grow, learn, and build trust. In order to be open and honest with someone, that person must be someone you can trust, will be understanding, and not make you feel bad or shame you. It is scary for all of us to be open because that makes us vulnerable. However, being vulnerable with your spouse is what connects you on a more intimate level and helps us to understand why we are the way that we are. We all have experienced someone making us feel bad for making a mistake.

You must understand that making a mistake does not define who you are or decrease your worth. When you are willing to learn from the mistake, you become wiser. After all, some of the greatest wisdom comes from experience and mistakes. The one thing my husband and I have never done since the day we met is ever made the other feel bad for making a mistake or for our pasts. Instead, we realized what went wrong, fixed it, let it go, and moved forward. I see so many people clinging to a silly mistake their spouse made, holding it over their head, or constantly bringing it up time and time again. This will breed resentment on both ends, so it is important to know how to let it go, forgive, and move forward.

One of the most important keys to marriage is being self-aware. Know your own flaws, know when you are in the wrong, know your own triggers, and know why you react the way you do. When two people who are self-aware come together and get married, it is beautiful, and it is so vital in such a way that it will avoid conflict most of the time. I can count only on one hand the number of times my husband and I have had a fight, and this is due to self-awareness. We immediately know when we are wrong; we immediately apologize, and we immediately self-correct. Let go of the pride. Let go of your ego. Those two things are not welcome in a marriage. Be humble, be genuinely sorry when you should be, and always forgive your spouse. Let it go, and do not bring it up again and hold it over their head. This will create so much resentment and make your spouse pull back and cause a distance between you. Making someone feel bad for something they already feel bad enough about and are sorry about will damage your connection. Your spouse will be less likely to come to you or talk to you in the future in fear of getting talked down on or yelled at. In marriage, when you can see your own flaws, and you come together, it makes you better together, and you are able to hold yourself accountable to each other and to God.

Imagine you are a kid again, and your parents yelled at you because you forgot to put away the milk, and it went bad. "How can you forget to put away the milk you know better, and now I have to go and get new milk!" You feel bad about it because you did not mean to, but you feel even worse because your parents yelled at you and made you feel small because of it. Instead, your parent could have had grace and said with a loving tone, "It's okay. It is not a big deal. We can get another gallon of milk. Just try to remember next time to put it away." That sounds a lot better, right? You would be less likely to make the mistake again, and you are not dwelling on it because you were not made to feel bad.

While this example may seem silly, it is relevant. If you did not like getting yelled at as a kid, you will not like getting yelled at as an adult, and I guarantee your spouse does not like getting yelled at either. This example shows how we can react to any situation. We can choose anger, or we can choose grace and love. I can bet you 100 percent of the time, your spouse will respond positively to grace and love and will produce a more trusting and intimate connection between you both. Knowing how to speak to and react to your spouse makes all the difference in how they will speak and react to you. Remember to focus on your mindset and ask yourself, "Is this really worth getting that upset about?"

One circumstance I have noticed that is common (we are guilty of it too) is giving your spouse a hard time about not doing something they were supposed to. You feel like you are the one doing everything around the house, and you asked your spouse to do this one chore—let's say dishes, for example. The dishes never gets done, and you give your spouse a hard time. In your mind, you are rightfully upset because you asked them to do it, and they said they would. What you don't see or understand is that your spouse intended to, but they had a long, stressful day at work. Your spouse came home exhausted mentally, physically, and emotionally and just needed to wind down and rest. Your spouse may have even planned to do it the next day because they know in their mind you asked them to do it. Giving them a hard time about it can cause them to shut down, decrease their motivation for the present and future, and then they are less likely to do what was asked. Instead of jumping to conclusions, always consider all scenarios or reasonings. They could have simply forgotten too, but that is no reason to get overly upset.

One day, I was having a bad day myself, and I saw the dishes in the sink that were supposed to get done. My first reaction was to get upset. The Lord spoke to me and said one word: "don't." I realized that my husband likely had a stressful day of work and was too tired. Instead, my attitude changed, and I happily did them myself to take the stress off him. I took that with me, and that is something I work on every day still for any situation. If you are looking at the dirty dishes in the sink and seeing a negative situation every time, it will cause a negative response. However, if you see the dirty dishes in the sink, and we positively, lovingly consider the reasons why they are still there, it changes your attitude. It changes your heart and therefore helps avoid a petty conflict that neither you nor your spouse would care to have. When you start to try to understand a scenario from every perspective, you are less likely to lose your cool and have unnecessary (or even misdirected) anger or frustration toward your life partner.

My grandfather gave us a list of things to do before we got married. One of them was to read the book *The 5 Love Languages* by Gary Chapman together, and we did. I highly recommend everyone reads this book as it is so helpful in any relationship. I already knew about the five love languages; however, I had never read that book before, and it taught me so much. This book can help you to truly understand each other and learn your own love language, as well as your spouse's. This will help you know how they receive love and how you yourself receive love as each of us receives love differently. This book also talks about children and learning your child's love language, which is important as each child is different in how they receive love.

Knowing the love languages can help relationship you have with anyone in your life. You must understand what makes a person feel loved because it may not be the same as what makes you feel loved. The way you think, feel, or perceive is not always the same as how someone else thinks, feels, or perceives. Once you understand that, you can learn how to understand others, especially your spouse! Men and women think differently, and we make up for what the other lacks so we can complement each other and be one together in marriage, which is absolutely beautiful!

When you take the time to learn from each other, it gives you the ability to serve each other properly (which we will discuss in the next chapter). Knowing each other's love language is imperative, but also learning and knowing each other's triggers and boundaries is just as important. You must respect boundaries, as well as know what is triggering your spouse.

For example, I am a very sensitive person. I always have been since I was a little girl. My main love language is words of affirmation because I need that affirmation to feel like I am doing enough or good enough. This stems from my past. Multiple people have invalidated my feelings or made me feel bad for having feelings. Has anyone ever told you to stop being so sensitive or overreacting when you were just genuinely trying to explain how you felt, and they did not understand? That is what had happened to me multiple times in my past, and I am still healing and growing from that.

I married a needle in the haystack. My husband is so patient and so understanding. He is also a jokester, a very funny one. There was one time I was so hangry; it was like I was not even myself. I just wanted some Olive Garden breadsticks. We were driving, and he said to me, "We are going to eat, and then we are going to stop at the store for a few things. Yay." It was winter. Winter is cold, and winter is not my season. I do not like going to the store in the winter. In fact, I do not even like to leave my house in the winter. I do not enjoy being cold, and I will complain when I am cold. I was willing to leave for Olive Garden breadsticks that day but not for a trip to the store. The hangry brat I was being sighed and said, "Do we have to?"

He said to me, "Stop being a baby."

This innocent man, all jokes, and not even in the slightest bit ever serious when he says anything like that had no idea what my response was going to be. My hangry and hormonal emotions spoke for me, and I said, "Why are you so mean?" I almost cried. I was huffing and puffing like a teenage girl. I was acting like a baby, and I knew that immediately, and I apologized (after I was two Olive Garden breadsticks in to ease the hanger). Where did this reaction stem from? Yes, I was hangry. Yes, I was emotional. But that is not all of it.

Even knowing my husband, who does not have any hostility toward me in him, I still took offense because I was triggered from being called a baby in the past when I was genuinely trying to show raw emotion, felt belittled, and like my feelings did not matter. It is a misdirected emotional reaction that I felt so bad for. This happens so often in relationships, and we often do not think about finding out why our spouse is acting or reacting the way that they are. You have to understand triggers, where they come from, and why so that we can avoid getting upset at each other. Instead, we can have empathy and know it likely is coming from an issue within ourselves that we can learn to heal together so the past does not bleed onto our present. This also helps us to know our spouse's triggers are so we can respond accordingly or understand why our spouse is reacting the way that they are. Be slow to anger with your spouse just as God is slow to anger with us. Psalm 86:15 says, "But you, O Lord, are a God merciful and gracious, slow to anger, and abounding in steadfast love and faithfulness."

Another way my husband shows words of affirmation to me is through his words and compliments. There has not been one single day since we have been together that he has not told me I am beautiful—every single day. He has not missed one day. Do you know what that has motivated me to do every day as well?—tell him how handsome he is—every day. He was the first one to say, "I love you." I was too scared, but he was not. Ever since the first time he said it, there has not been a day that has gone by that we have not said it to each other. Never stop telling your spouse you love them, and never stop showing it each day!

To learn about your spouse on a deeper level, you must also pay attention to their perception. Men and women tend to perceive differently. Learning how our spouse perceives versus assuming how they perceive can make or break the direction your marriage is heading. Assuming anything is dangerous in general, but assuming how your spouse perceives you or a situation can cause issues. How do you learn how our spouse perceives something? That is the million-dollar question with an answer you would never expect! The answer is, ask them! Crazy, right?

If I was asked to provide just one piece of marriage advice to a married couple, I would pick this: Your spouse does not perceive the way you do, and you do not perceive the same way your spouse does. Learn to perceive everything from each other's perspectives, and learn empathy. Be able to place yourself in your spouse's shoes the best that you can.

Before I get into an example to explain perception, I want to explain what I mean by perception. We all know perception is how we view, see, understand, or interpret something. The things in marriage we perceive can be tone in the way you say something, facial expressions, body language, or an action for some examples. In the example I provided above, I assumed my husband's comment to me was hostile; however, he was just joking around, like he always does, and I was reacting defensively based on a trigger.

The biggest one that I think (here I am assuming when I just told you not to assume… joking of course) gets my husband and others is my resting facial expressions. I don't have the friendliest resting face. In fact, I have had several people tell me they thought I hated them or thought I was mean because of my face. This was their perception because of my facial expression, when really, I am very friendly and kind. But what they usually don't know or understand is that I am very introverted sometimes. I also tend to get stuck in my head, thinking about something, and my facial expressions change based on that thought, so it may seem to someone else's perception that I am angry, sad, or mad. The point is, sometimes how we perceive someone's facial expression is not always accurate or aimed directly at you personally.

I have two examples to describe perception in marriage. The first one is how we view and see marriage. When my grandfather asked my husband why he wanted to marry me, his response was, "Because I love her." My grandfather responded, "Love is more than just a feeling, and love is what you do." Oh, he terrified my (not-yet but almost) husband that day. My husband perceived it as an interrogation, but my grandfather was planting a seed of understanding into both of us about what marriage and love is.

My perception of marriage has always been two people who love each other that have the following characteristics: loyalty, respect, humor, grace, honesty, motivation, work ethic, morals and principles to stand on, fun, selflessness, honor, love for others/animals, and so on. My husband's perception of marriage was on the same page as mine by the time we were meeting with my grandfather before we got married.

Both of our perceptions were somewhat validated yet also strengthened both of our perceptions on marriage. We realized that becoming one together is more than just words we read; it is supposed to be an unbreakable bond. Marriage is a miracle because you become one! Matthew 19:6 says, "So they are no longer two, but one flesh. What, therefore, God has joined together, let no man separate." Just as Jesus and the church (His bride) is one, so is man and wife as marriage is supposed to mirror our relationship and unity with Jesus.

The more both of your hearts become like Jesus's heart, the closer you become, and the more you will have the ability to understand each other's perceptions, which then strengthens your connection in marriage. If you have the same perception on marriage as your spouse, you can be on and stay on the same page throughout your marriage.

My second example for perception in marriage is how we can differently view many aspects of life. The example I am going to use to hopefully make it simple to understand is the perception of cleanliness in the home. I know it is such a shocker that I am bringing up chores again, but for each scenario, this seems to be the best way for me to explain.

I used to always be a neat freak my whole life. I wanted everything super clean and organized. It caused a lot of anxiety in me. After years of always cleaning up after everyone else/pets or making sure everything was perfect, I started to realize how unhealthy it was for me. I started to back down and not let it affect me like it did before. I still have my struggles sometimes, but I still like to say, a house that does not look lived in is not worth living in so I don't feel bad if not everything is super clean.

My whole neat freak phase ended about a year before I met my husband. I thought I could never meet anyone who loved cleanliness as much as I did until I met my husband, who was even *more* of a clean freak than me. My definition of dirty and his definition of dirty are completely different. How I perceive dirty is how he perceives filthy. This is not a bad thing at all. In fact, it challenged me to learn his cleaning standards and to become better. I had to find a balance between making sure I do keep up with his definition of clean while also not falling back into an unhealthy clean freak pattern that caused me anxiety. We found a happy medium.

I don't notice when certain things are dirty because I don't perceive it as dirty, and I had to learn how to perceive it from my husband's perception. What is frustrating to him might not be frustrating to me. What is frustrating to me might not be frustrating to him. However, the point is to learn each other's perspectives. If it does not look dirty to you, but it does to your spouse, clean it anyway. Am I perfect at that yet?—not at all, but I am trying and constantly learning. This is how I encourage it to be for any situation. If you perceive something differently than your spouse, try to perceive it their way, or at least try to understand their perception just as you would want them to understand yours. Celebrate your differences in perspective because another perspective can be a blessing and push you to grow. It is great that you think or see differently so we can learn to see life from a different perspective!

To tie together perception, I want to talk about morals and principles. One of the most important pieces of advice I could give anyone in a relationship or marriage is to learn what each other's morals and principles are, if there even is any (tip: there always should be). It is so important to have morals and principles you both stand on or agree on (all the time), otherwise it will not be a fun marriage, and there will be a lot of hurt and disappointment.

What is the reasoning behind morals and principles?—to have a strong foundation of values on which you always stand and follow, regardless of the circumstances. If you are not equally yoked when it comes to beliefs, the relationship is already on its way to failure. Why is this? If you justify an action or opinion based on what you believe, but your spouse believes otherwise, there is no agreement, which will lead to conflict eventually.

The best way I can explain it is through an example relating to adultery. In Matthew 24:27–28, Jesus said, "You have heard that it was said, you shall not commit adultery. But I say to you that everyone who looks at a woman with lustful intend has already committed adultery with her in his heart." What was Jesus saying? There are a lot of ways this verse has been interpreted; however, the way the Lord has revealed the meaning to me is what I will explain. He was not saying this to condemn; He was revealing to us the condition of our own heart. He was saying that if a man is looking at another woman with lust, that the act of adultery is already something that has been planted in your own mind/heart. Think of it more as a wake-up call to get your heart and thoughts in check. I agree with this verse wholeheartedly, and it is another reminder to guard our hearts and minds seriously. I bring this verse up because of the way the world views or justifies adultery. I used to think like the world, so I know both sides. This is the question I hear a lot of people talk about: What is considered cheating? Well, the verse makes that very clear; however, everyone would be divorced and single for looking at someone else in lust while in a relationship. I don't want you to misunderstand the point or the principle of this message. I want to emphasize what I said earlier; Jesus was showing us that even looking in lust is committing adultery on our heart because we, in our fleshly and sinful human nature, tend to end up acting on thoughts. Most actions require aforethought. The example here is adultery. Chances are that most affairs required the thought of the act before the actual act. If you believe in monogamy, and your spouse believes in open marriage, the marriage is not going to work.

How does the world answer what is considered cheating? Maybe the better question is, What does the world not consider cheating? I have heard all of it. "Well, we were just flirting through text. We never did anything." "Well, we only kissed. We did not do anything else." I think a lot of people consider cheating to be physical, but it can be emotional too. One of the most beautiful gifts that God gave us is free will. We can choose what we want to believe in and what we want to do. That free will can really get us humans into trouble. God gave us all the choice to choose to follow Him or not.

If you are not already married, before you get married, ask what your partner's definition of cheating and loyalty is. It will tell you a lot about where they are mentally, emotionally, and spiritually. It is important to have these conversations before marriage and to make sure you are on the same page to be able to share your beliefs and why you believe that way. There is no room for anyone else in marriage, only commitment to each other with God guiding the marriage. Adultery is the example I chose to use, but make sure to ask where your partner stands on morals and principles. If you are already married, you can still have these discussions of course!

The world tends to refer to adultery as an affair, but another word for this is infidelity or, in other words, a breaking of trust. Anything you must hide from your spouse that can break your trust, stay away from it. I notice in a lot of relationships hiding phones and passwords. It is strange to me because while we do not have the desire or feel the need to go through each other's phones, we have access and passwords because we trust each other so much. Proverbs 3:3–4 says, "Let love and faithfulness never leave you; bind them around your neck, write them on the tablet of your heart. Then you will win favor and a good name in the sight of God and man."

When my husband and I discussed what we expected in marriage, we agreed and respected each other's personal feelings. I think we both had reached a point where we wanted to seek truth in life and would accept nothing less than the truth, even when the truth is a hard pill to swallow. Seeking truth, speaking truth, and knowing truth is peace. Trust in marriage makes for a peaceful marriage. I always liked the saying, "if you wouldn't want someone to know what you did, don't do it." Guilt will destroy you and your marriage, as well as breed paranoia, conflict, and emotional turmoil.

When my husband and I first got together, two of the most important moral values we agreed on were trust and loyalty. These are two values that it seems almost rare to come by these days. You see affairs, lying, and cheating almost glorified in media/music/real life. When we met, we were at a point in our life where we were ready to have a partner in life that you could count on, rely on, and trust completely in. Trust is always earned, and it takes time to build trust, but it takes as little as a second to lose.

The first two years together were not easy. We had baggage from our pasts that we tried our hardest not to carry over, but the effects of that baggage were obvious in both of us. The baggage still did affect us in some ways. We spent two years building trust, helping each other heal, and becoming best friends that we could be vulnerable to and ourselves around because of how much trust we had built. This took a lot of effort and patience, and it was worth all of it.

The best part of the first two years of our relationship was the fact that all of the work we put in and all of the healing and growth we did together set us up for a healthy future together. It felt like all of that work actually made our relationship, and now marriage, stronger and honestly easier. We have no trust issues. We are both self-aware. We apologize. We forgive. We don't fight or yell. (We never really did. We both dislike conflict and yelling.) We can read each other so well that we know how to resolve a problem before it is a problem or even avoid having a problem at all. It almost feels like it is too good to be true, or at least it probably seems that way to the outside world. The truth is, it is not too good to be true. Our marriage is the result of two people (from the beginning) working hard to really learn about each other, genuinely wanting the best for each other, and wanting that long-lasting marriage hard enough to put the time and energy into one another. Again, marriage is not always easy, but it is one of the most rewarding and beautiful gifts to have. I thank God every day for giving me the husband He did because I could not imagine life without him or with anyone else.

Wisdom and knowledge make you richer than money ever could. Your spouse will have wisdom you may not have, so make sure you learn from one another. Listen to what your spouse has to say, and really reflect on the wisdom they share with you. One of the most beautiful parts of marriage is learning from each other and applying the knowledge you share.

I want to end this chapter with this: Do not stop learning about your spouse. Keep learning about them every single day.

CHAPTER 2

Growing Together

A great marriage takes two people who humbly know they are not perfect, are able to self-examine themselves every day (and allow God to examine you) while also understanding and knowing their spouse is not perfect so the two of you can grow together. After all, not one of us humans are perfect, and we all need grace and understanding. It is uncomfortable to examine yourself at first and allow God to examine you, but it is needed to help you grow so you can receive the knowledge and wisdom needed to apply it to your marriage. Put aside your ego and your pride. Once you admit you are broken and imperfect, you can give it to Jesus so He can take the weight of our burdens, and He works on our imperfections. Philippians 1:6 reads, "And I am sure of this, that He who began a good work in you will bring it to completion at the day of Jesus Christ." Once Jesus starts that good work in you, He promises to finish it. And when that is being done in you and your spouse, you will see it in your marriage.

I tell everyone all the time about how much I love my husband and how he is the best husband I could ever have. I fall in love with him more and more each day. I never knew such a love was possible because I never experienced it before. The television does not do any good at representing a healthy and fun marriage either. I had felt love before but not like this. I always give advice to those searching for their person to stop searching. Don't search, just live your life, grow, let God do the work in you to prepare you for your spouse. God will place that person in your life when you least expect it because that is what He did for me, and that is what He has done for so many others that I have talked to. Oftentimes, God is growing you and preparing you so that when the time is right, and your spouse comes into your life, you will be able to continue to grow, but now, it will be the two of you growing together. The typical response I get is sometimes an eye roll, maybe an "I know, but what if I don't look, and I miss out on finding them?" I promise you will not miss out on finding them. In fact, they will likely find you. If I know anything for sure, it is that God's timing is always perfect, whether we acknowledge it was His doing or not. Another one of my favorites to say is, "when you meet your spouse, you will know they are the one." I love saying that because I was the person that used to eye roll at that one. Anytime anyone said that to me, I was so negative. "Yeah, right, whatever. That is so cliché and so dumb." I love that I have become the one saying it when I used to believe that it was bologna. Funny how life works, right?

You will tend to learn that the wise advice we were given by someone ends up being advice we share when we have learned the truth behind it or experience it for ourselves. If someone has wisdom or advice (especially when it includes something that will help you, others, and not hurt anyone else), listen to it, soak it in, think about it, apply it, and you will watch yourself grow and your life change. Watch your marriage succeed. On the contrary, you must use discernment and take some advice with a grain of salt or ignore it. Growing includes learning ourselves and learning who you let influence your life as well.

If you do, confide in a friend about an issue you are having with your spouse. For us, we prefer to keep ours private and between us and God, which works for us. However, having a friend you can trust or confide in is helpful sometimes, just please be wise in who you share with or go to for advice. Your friend's advice can be helpful or harmful. I will use a made-up example for this.

Example problem: You and your spouse are fighting a lot and cannot seem to agree on much. You feel like this is causing you to lose connection and intimacy emotionally. You decide you want to ask your married friend for some advice since you and your spouse are unable to get on the same page, and you both feel distant.

Example of good advice to the problem: I think you should find the root cause of what is causing the fighting. Are one or both of you stressed? Is there a lack of communication or miscommunication? I think you should both sit down and be open about how each of you are feeling. Listen to understand, not to speak. Be vulnerable and honest, and talk it out. Maybe you just need to understand what the other is going through in order to understand why you are having the issues so you can tackle it together.

Example of bad advice to the problem: Your marriage sounds like it is failing, and maybe you should forget them and find someone else. It does not sound like it is fixable, and there are so many other people out there.

If you are someone who wants your marriage to work because you love your spouse and your marriage, you are probably thinking that bad advice is not what you would want to hear. This will likely discourage you and plant seeds of doubt and failure into your mind and poison your soul and marriage even more. When you actively go to someone you trust seeking advice, you need to be and want to be encouraged, but you also need truth spoken to you with love and grace.

The world does often say, if there are issues, find someone else. Guess what? You will have issues with someone else too. Relationships and marriages are not always fun and happy. Marriage is work (you can't get lazy). The truth is, marriage is a covenant between two people who made vows and promises to one another (remember, in sickness and in health, for richer and for poorer, and so on). Marriage can be messy and hard. I like to think of it as marrying your best friend, who you are willing to work through everything with. Climb every mountain together, experience every high and low together, and work every problem out together. You are a team, tackling the problem and learning how to get through it together. Don't let others plant seeds of doubt, hate, negativity into your mind and heart. Be filled with seeds of love, encouragement, and hope and watch your marriage bear fruit. Be careful who you trust in, and be mindful of the advice you are given. It is important to use discernment and listen to what the Lord is telling you. What is normally labeled as your gut feeling is the Lord speaking, so always listen to that when it comes to listening to outside opinions!

Growth comes from learning. My husband and I are both coachable individuals. My husband was the most "I want to learn" person I have ever met in my entire life from the very beginning. That is contagious, and it spreads to me like wildfire quickly. (Side note: Positivity is contagious, but negativity is just as contagious. Choose your wildfire wisely.) We are both actively seeking knowledge, wanting and willing to learn about anything and everything, and we both want to become more Christlike in our hearts. This helps our marriage stay healthy because, while neither of us are perfect, we have the tools, the openness to humbly help us tackle any issue, talk through any problem, or show grace and understanding during bad days. One of the biggest parts of growth in marriage is learning how to listen. Your spouse is likely telling you what bothers them, and it is important to listen to everything they say and make the necessary changes.

If one of us is discouraged, stressed, upset, you name it, the other is there to be the voice of reason and the calm in the storm. If I only have 20 percent to give one day (which is my 100 percent that I can give that day), my husband is the 80 percent that day and vice versa. I can tell you that there is one thing I give absolutely 0 percent to, and that is laundry (not very wifely of me I know). I hate laundry, not dislike—hate with a capital HATE. This is something I am still working on. I have no motivation for laundry, but my husband is the king of laundry. The thought of laundry makes me tired. You know what my husband's response to that is? "Why it is not so easy? All you do is throw it in and switch it over." You know what I think out loud when he says that? "No, honey, you have to fold it and put it away, and that is the worst part." Guess who ends up being the one that folds it and puts it away. You guessed it: me—which is hilarious because we laugh about it all the time.

We tackle things as a team. I love to cook, and I cook dinner almost every day. My husband does the dishes when I cook. When he cooks, I do the dishes. When he does the laundry, I fold it and put it away. (I don't complain once either. Can you sense the sarcasm? I am working on that too.) One time, before my husband was leaving for work, he came up to me all smiles, like he was so excited, like he was being so romantic. He looked me in the eye and said, "Babe, there is a surprise for you on the bed." I was so excited. Was it food? Was it a new pair of work-from-home sweatpants or leggings? I was close. It was the laundry (my work-from-home leggings and sweatpants), waiting to get folded. I laughed so hard, and I will never forget that! He makes something I hate doing fun, and that is something I admire and love about him. All jokes aside, we really do make it a priority to work as a team and make the workload even. I like to say to him, "I want to be something that makes life less stressful for you, not more stressful," and I believe that is one of the keys toward a healthy and happy marriage. I hate the saying "happy wife, happy life," and he says that all the time to joke with me. I promise you, that saying is not doing anyone any good. I prefer the saying "happy spouse, happy house." You cannot win unless you are both happy.

We all know the famous saying or what is often referred to as the golden rule that says, "treat others how you want to be treated." I think we are all taught that in elementary school. This problem I do have with this phrase is, it depends on if you look at it from a relativism perspective or an absolute perspective. As followers of Christ, we look it as an absolute perspective, grounded on the truth of the Word. With that being said, it is important to understand the context of this phrase as being absolute as it relates to marriage.

Treat your spouse how you want to be treated by your spouse. Always remember, your spouse is just as human as you are, and they are not always going to get it right. If you show grace to your spouse, they are likely to return grace. If you show anger toward your spouse, they are likely going to return anger. Humans are very social and influential creatures. If you have heard the saying "you are who you hang out with," this is correct because it is in our nature to influence each other. If you are not normally an angry person, but your spouse is constantly yelling at you, you are likely going to get pushed over your limit and yell back. If your spouse is always seeing the positive in every negative situation, you are likely going to start seeing the positive in negative situations as well. In a marriage, you truly do reap what you sow. It is your choice to decide which seeds you plant into one another and which seeds you allow to grow within yourself. A good verse to remember and apply is Ephesians 4:2–3: "Be completely humble and gentle; be patient with one another in love. Make every effort to keep the unity of the Spirit through the bond of peace."

There are many signs you are actively growing together with your spouse. I am the type of person who apologizes for everything to everyone in general, even if I did not do anything wrong. To make it funny: "Sorry for breathing your air." It is hard sometimes to apologize when we are wrong. We all have that sense of pride. However, that pride cannot come between you and your spouse. Your pride is not more important than your spouse. Learn to swallow your pride willingly and lovingly. If you are wrong, admit it, apologize, and mean it. Then work on it.

No, your wife is not nagging you because you forgot to do something again. She is frustrated because you have not listened multiple times, done what you have promised you would, and feels unheard and unimportant. No, your husband is not being a jerk when he tells you to calm down because you have an attitude because you are having a bad day or hormonal. Remember, learn the root of your own reaction, understand it, and admit when you are wrong. If you say something like, "You are right, honey. I am sorry I have been having a bad and emotional day," watch how positive the response is. When you apologize, own your own behavior and offer an explanation (not an excuse). Your spouse will be much more understanding and likely mirror that when they are in the wrong. It is also wise to never say or do anything when you are angry. Anger clouds judgment, and you can never take back words or actions. Proverbs 18:21 says, "Death and life are in the power of the tongue and those who love it will eat its fruits." Our words have a lot of power, so be careful with what you say. I remember the nicest things anyone has ever said to me, but I also remember the most hurtful things anyone has ever said to me. Be sure you are saying words that breathe life into your spouse and encourage growth.

When your spouse genuinely admits they are wrong and apologizes, forgive them. They already know they are wrong; they feel bad enough without you overexplaining why they are wrong. The next step is to move past it. Don't bring it up again or hold it over their head. Have you ever felt good by anyone constantly reminding you of your mistakes or making you feel bad? I don't think anyone has. Learn and grow together from it openly. If you notice a pattern, and the behavior does not change, absolutely address it graciously and go from there. My husband and I reached the point of growth where if we apologize to each other for something, the mistake or what caused the upset is likely never going to happen again. This is exactly the goal. This is not to say you will ever reach perfection because you won't. The point is to be willing to change, work on it, and to show grace and understanding toward one another, and you can and will be able to grow to work through anything together. Your spouse will appreciate and recognize the difference.

You are not always going to get it right, but one of the most beautiful parts of marriage is being best friends that continue to grow and learn together with grace, patience, and understanding. When you encourage your spouse's growth, you are bound to willingly grow yourself. Never stop growing together and building each other up. First Thessalonians 5:11 says, "Therefore encourage one another and build each other up, just as in fact you are doing."

CHAPTER 3

Quality Time Together

There is a substantial difference between spending quantity time with someone and spending quality time with someone. When it comes to your marriage, quality time is imperative; I will argue daily. While life can get busy, and you may not get as much time as we would like with your spouse, the quality of the time you do share with your spouse makes all the difference.

Some personal examples of quality time together include making sure to really talk to each other deeply daily, attentively listening to your spouse when they speak, or doing an activity together you both enjoy (even if it is just watching your favorite TV show). Doing anything together that is important to your spouse makes for great quality time together.

Laugh together, and make everything you do together fun, even if it is something that is not usually fun (such as cleaning or, in my case, laundry). If you are looking for more quality time or more laughter in your marriage, it starts with you. You have the choice to make any situation fun or to make it miserable. If you are looking for more quality time with your spouse, instead of complaining or waiting for your spouse to make the effort first, plan something that will give you that quality time you need.

My husband and I have worked opposite shifts for a few years now. I am halfway through my shift before he even leaves for work, and I am in bed asleep by the time he gets home. This has given us only weekends and his lunch break to see each other through the week. Instead of seeing that as an obstacle, we have planned specific ways to spend quality time together each day. I cook dinner after work so he can come home on his lunch break to a home-cooked meal, and we have that hour to be able to talk if need to, to have dinner together, and to catch an episode of whatever show we are watching at the time. Every Friday night in the winter is date night. Whatever the circumstances may be, we have always put each other first and made sure to make that time for each other. Every marriage and relationship has that option too! You are too busy if you don't, and it is important to make necessary changes to have the time for your spouse. A spouse that feels neglected will pull away, and before you know it, you have slowly lost motivation and connection, and that is what we try to avoid!

This is not to say that all your time has to be with your spouse of course! Friends, family, and "you" time are so important too! Your spouse always comes first; however, it is important to allow them to have that time with others or themselves, if needed. Finding the appropriate balance that works for your marriage is key. For us, with our work schedules, we get our designated alone time to recharge each day because of our opposite schedules. It is necessary to take that time if you need it so you can make sure you are not running on empty, so you are able to pour into your spouse. After all, none of us can pour into anyone else if we, ourselves, are completely drained.

If I have one piece of advice for husbands for quality time, it is this: You can miss the game for your wife. Before you throw this book out the window and stop reading, hear me out. This is not an attack! While I know there are controlling relationships out there, if you are not in one, your wife is pleading for quality time with you, so give it to her. I promise there will be other games to go to or watch, but the time your wife is desperate for in that moment is far more important than anything else. The same goes for wives. If your husband is asking you to miss something to spend important time with him (not in a "controlling way" context is everything), please listen to him and spend the time with him. I think we sometimes think our spouse is being needy or controlling, when really, they are trying to express their need for quality time with us. I will remind you of perspectives we talked about in the first chapter in order to help you understand what your spouse is actually trying to express to you. If you are having trouble understanding your spouse, pray on it. The Lord has never failed at helping me understand and see my husband's feelings or perspectives so I can better respond.

Life can be stressful. Bills add up, prices go up, unexpected emergencies or tragedies happen, and bad days at work are unavoidable, but how you deal with that stress together is what matters. Sometimes quality time is not always all fun. Sometimes it takes the time to discuss your stress, crying or venting and figuring out how to get through the problem together. It is making short-term and long-term goals together and holding each other accountable to make sure the goals can be attained together. The result of quality time is sometimes figuring out along the way how strong your marriage really is because you have a teammate getting through all of the struggles with you instead of against you. Be vulnerable to your spouse during your quality time. If you are both able to be vulnerable, I can guarantee, your marriage will grow stronger because both of you were able to let the guards down. If you are not married yet, be vulnerable before you are married because, like us, we were vulnerable before, and it changed our hearts and minds to make the decision to get married.

It is important to be able to get away together from the stress and worries of life sometimes, not run away. Please don't run away from your problems; they will be waiting when you return. My husband and I essentially made an invisible pact to work hard to make vacations possible every year in the future when we first met. We both love traveling, have always loved traveling, but never could afford it in the past.

A lot of our quality time after our first couple years together was spent working on financial discipline together. I will discuss finances in depth further in a later chapter. We wanted vacations and we wanted a house. The Lord promised that to us, but He also told me what we had to do in order for the promise to be fulfilled. We spent two years paying off debt, cutting back on going out, and saving money. I will admit, one of those two years was the pandemic lockdowns, so we were forced into saving that year. The pandemic year was also an awesome quality time year for us. We really got to create visions for our future together, made plans financially, and we got to spend lots of quality time with the kids having game nights. The point here is, do not be discouraged by your current situation if you are unable to do what you would like to do for specific quality time together, such as vacation. You can spend quality time planning and working together for those goals, and that quality time is just as precious together.

Quality time does not require money or the perfect life; it just requires two happy people who love each other that want to spend time together. It is important to note not to work too hard or too much because the stress will bleed into your marriage. Work hard, just do not overwork yourself or allow the stress of work to come home with you.

Be patient because good things take time to earn, and God always provides when the time is just right! When you are financially stable enough or able to, absolutely take the vacation or take that weekend getaway. Being able to do all of this has helped us tremendously to make it a goal to take a weekend getaway when we can and try to do at least one or two vacations per year. This has helped us get away from stress so we can have fun, clear our minds, come back feeling refreshed, but most importantly, have that quality time together.

Quality time and date nights do not have to cost money at all. Quality time is free. You can drive somewhere for the day, even the beach. You can have a game night, movie night, and cook dinner at home. Money cannot provide the amount of appreciation and growth that quality time provides.

I hear a lot of talk about how often couples should plan date nights. Of course, it is based off a number of factors, as we sort of touched on before, but it most importantly is what works for you and your spouse. I would like to suggest anywhere from once a week to at least once a month. For us, we prefer to do it at least once a week. Date night at home is still date night; it does not have to cost a dime!

We live in a world where we are so connected to the Internet with our smart phones. That it is often hard to disconnect. We even struggle with that but are fully aware of it. During date nights or any quality time with your spouse, turn off your phones or just don't touch them. Give each other your undivided attention, and listen to each other so you can be more connected to your spouse than your device.

One of my favorite things to ask a couple that has been married for thirty-plus years is, What has made your marriage last long and what makes you still happy? The most common answer I have received is, they always make sure to have quality time together through all of their years of marriage. The main takeaway I want you to have from this chapter is to always make time for meaningful, quality time with your spouse. Romans 12:10 is one of my favorite verses to remind myself of daily. This verse reads, "Be devoted to one another in love. Honor one another above yourselves."

CHAPTER 4

Communication

There are two main reasons for divorce I have noticed and learned about: lack of communication and finances. I will discuss finances in the next chapter. Communication is vital in any relationship we have with anyone we love. When we do not communicate our feelings, perceptions, ideas, boundaries, triggers, and so on, we are setting our relationship up for conflict that can be easily avoided.

Our mind is our own worst enemy sometimes. Our thoughts can play tricks on us and make us believe something that is not true or lead us to make assumptions. One fact to always remember is, we cannot read anyone's mind, so your spouse certainly cannot read your mind. Since humans are social beings, we can pick up on signals through body language, tone, and wording. However, we cannot make assumptions based on those alone. While they are great indicators to show what our spouse is feeling, they do not provide all of the facts. The best way to fully read what our spouse is communicating through their body language or lack thereof is to ask questions.

If your spouse is quiet and looks upset, do not always assume they are mad at you or that you did something wrong. Instead, ask them what is wrong. The number of times my husband and I have thought the other was upset with the other is too many to count. Most of the time, it is one of us stressed or upset about something else, and we are thinking about it so deeply that it affects our mood or keeps us quiet. When you ask, listen while they communicate to you and understand why your spouse is acting or feeling the way they do. It can avoid giving into the feelings of assumption and creating false scenarios in your head. If you make the decision that your spouse is mad at you and act out on it, it can cause conflict and could potentially add more stress onto your spouse. On the contrary, if you ask what is wrong, and they are upset with you, ask them graciously why, apologize, and ask genuinely for ways to fix it. Your spouse needs to feel comfortable communicating what is wrong, how you or anything else made them feel, communicating their feelings, and explaining their requests.

The way you communicate with your spouse matters. The tone in which you communicate and how you interpret tone is imperative to be aware of. If you communicate in a condescending or sarcastic tone to your spouse, they are certainly likely to react negatively. However, it is also important to note that sometimes tone can be misdirected. If your spouse is using a tone that you take as disrespectful to you, acknowledge it but also use empathy and ask yourself, "Could this be misdirected at me because my spouse is stressed about something else?" Most of the times, my husband and I have used a tone the other did not like; it came from a place of stress or hurt that did not come from the other. This is another example, as I have stressed already multiple times, of having grace, empathy, and understanding with your spouse. I believe, a lot of issues I have witnessed in marriages originate from misunderstood tone and misdirected negative tone. If you are both able to question and see the bigger picture behind tone, whether directly or indirectly toward you, and be able talk about it right away, your marriage will be less likely to lack the communication it needs.

Appreciation is a miracle worker in marriage. If you do not believe me, try it for yourself. My husband and I appreciate everything about each other. We do not just think about appreciation, we speak it. We both grew in this way together without even talking about the concept of showing appreciation. We just lived and saw how it worked. It takes little to no effort to appreciate your spouse. When you appreciate your spouse, you motivate them daily to keep on doing what they are doing *for* you. So if you want your spouse to keep doing anything for you with joy and love in their heart, tell them you appreciate what they have done, thank them, and show you appreciate them by returning the acts of service.

I mentioned earlier how I hate doing laundry. Do you know how my husband gets me to do it even if I don't want to?—appreciation, tone, and wording. "Babe, can you please put our laundry in? I did not have time today, and I appreciate it." What is my response? "Of course, I will I love you so much I would be glad to do that for you." I promise, if he ever said to me, "Put the laundry in. You never do the laundry. You are lazy, and the worst," I would never in a million years do the laundry for him. That statement would make me feel terrible and give me zero motivation to help. I doubt I would do anything for him, to be honest.

Present your requests with kindness, "please," and "thank you." Don't tear your spouse down. Build them up and positively position your requests. Make each other feel good, and you will have nothing but joy doing what the other asks of you. If your spouse does something for you, say "thank you. I appreciate you so much." My husband and I say "thank you" or "I appreciate you" to each other at least a minimum of six times a day. Even for something small, while I can argue the smallest things, are the biggest to me. He thanks me for cooking dinner every day, for giving him a shoulder massage every day, and for plugging in his headphones every day, for example. I tell him how much I appreciate him working hard, providing for us, mowing the lawn, and doing the dishes after I cook. What seems so small to be thankful or appreciative of really makes all the difference in the world when your spouse truly appreciates what you do and when you reciprocate the appreciation.

A big piece of communication that I have noticed is not normally discussed is listening. We can all talk and want to be heard ourselves, but it is important to make sure you listen to your spouse, not just listening to what they say but hearing what they are expressing. One of the biggest mistakes we, as imperfect humans, make is assuming what someone's words or body language means. If you are unsure what your spouse's words or body language is expressing, make sure to ask to understand. Assuming anything can cause an internal war within your mind and lead to overthinking.

A big puzzle piece that seems to be missing within most relationships and marriages is the lack of seeking to understand what your spouse is saying or expressing to you. I personally believe that the world has done a great job at socially engineering everyone to hide within themselves and not to speak about or communicate feelings because of fear. Fear has no place in marriage or in your life. Remember, the Bible reminds us 365 times, once for each day of the year, not to fear. There should be no fear with your spouse. Be able to and learn how to be completely emotionally naked with your spouse and know how to respond accordingly. Do not just listen to what your spouse is telling you, but hear what they are saying. Your spouse is likely always expressing their needs and feelings through words and body language; it is just up to you to understand the communication and act on it or to ask for clarification if you are not understanding.

Honesty is a key role in communication in marriage. Be honest, not with malice but with love. My husband and I like to have fun with each other. One example that is fun for him is, he will never tell me when I have food in my teeth. I remember the first time it happened, I asked him, "Why didn't you tell me I had something in my teeth?"

His response was, "Because it's funny."

To me, it is funny because it is something that makes him laugh, and we both are at an age where we don't necessarily care about something like that or what other people think. If you make it embarrassing, then it is embarrassing. I am an extremely embarrassing person and klutzy person, but I have and still am learning to embrace being a dork. (I got it from my mom, and I love my mom so much. She is the most amazing and funny mom I could have ever asked for.)

The reason I bring this example up is because, while something silly, like having something stuck in your teeth, may not be a big deal to us, it could be something big for someone else. You have a choice in how you react to something that might bother you a little more than it does to your spouse. I could have chosen to get upset and angry toward my husband, but instead I chose to make it funny too and not let it embarrass me. I like to be told if I have something in my teeth or on my face, but I chose to laugh about it. However, if it is something that really does get to your spouse, just let them know and understand, they take it differently than you do. Communication is full of choices, and you have to learn how to make the appropriate choice, putting your spouse's feelings above your own.

In marriage, it is important to be honest with your spouse, not just about the small things but the big things too. Your spouse is your best friend, your partner in life, and the one who is there for you no matter what. Don't let shame or fear stop you from being open and honest with your spouse. If something bothers you, tell them. If your spouse tells you something is bothering them, actually hear them, apologize, and work on it.

I will bring up laundry again (although, I cannot promise it will be the last time I bring it up). The laundry is not the point; it is the example. (Replace laundry with any other issue or thing, and you will understand the point.) If the laundry basket is full, I usually do not pay enough attention notice. I am a very routine person, which is a blessing sometimes, but also one of my downfalls that the Lord has been helping me work on for years. The laundry has never been a part of my routine; however, cooking and dishes are. If the laundry basket is full, and my husband notices after I have already put my dirty clothes in the basket for the day, what that communicates to him is that I hate laundry, and I avoided doing it, which is a fair assumption because I have communicated by hate for laundry. However, what he does not know is that I did not notice it was full because I threw my clothes in there when it was dark in the morning. Does he make me feel bad? No, he does not. He communicates to me to ask me to do it if I notice it is full, and I agree to because he is right, and I should because we are a team. This helps me to pay more attention and hear what he wants and needs from me. If you want your spouse to do more of something around the house, communicate it to them with love. If something upsets you, communicate the upset with love.

What you say, don't say, do, or don't do all communicate something to your spouse. Never assume that what your spouse is or is not communicating or that they are not doing their part is on purpose. This is another area where grace is imperative. Life can get busy, stressful, painful, and hard. If your spouse is not as active or doing as much of their part as you normally view, this is an unspoken communication to learn to pick up on. Are they working more hours? Is work stressful lately? Did they just experience a life hardship? How is their mental health lately? These are examples of questions to ask yourself before you react. I believe it is fair to say that the responsibility of being an adult, parent, full-time worker, friend, brother, sister, aunt, uncle, pet parent, or whatever other titles you may have are a lot to handle all at once. Life is overwhelming sometimes. And while the Lord is with us and provides us with the guidance we need, we fall short in our fallen human nature and sometimes forget to put our burdens on the Lord. Just as we discussed in previous chapters, being able to consider and understand our spouse's perception, feelings, and the ways they communicate all tie together.

I am so self-aware that I probably annoy others with it. I communicate and overexplain myself to everyone. I would not exchange that for anything though, and I will explain why. Through all of my traumas, experiences, and failures in life, I decided to learn the lesson and wisdom from all of them. One of the most important lessons I learned is how to communicate and understand communication, not just verbal but lack of verbal communication, as well as body language.

I used to apologize for overexplaining myself to others, but I am learning that it is perfectly okay. I tell my husband exactly why I act or react in a certain way to almost everything. He really does not have to ask me how I feel about anything because I certainly tell him all the time. I vent all my feelings to him about everything. This is a good reminder that Jesus wants us to vent all of our frustrations and feelings to Him too because He knows, feels, and cares for us. Husbands, let your wife talk to you about everything and anything without making her feel bad about it or acting annoyed. Wives, please do not be afraid to talk to your husband openly and honestly about everything. In order to clarify what I am trying to communicate (after all, this chapter is all about communication, right?), I will provide some examples in the next couple of paragraphs.

Have you ever had someone tell you they were going to show up for something or do something important to you, and they didn't, without any explanation or telling you why they were not able to make it? Your answer is likely yes. Why does this happen? I believe there are multiple reasons why. The least likely reason is they do not care about you nor care to explain themselves. (While this is rare, it does happen.) The most likely reasons are either something came up, and they could not let you know because they were dealing with the situation, or they were not feeling up to it emotionally or mentally and were too scared to let you know or let you down. There could be other factors or reasons, but those are the most likely examples. I used to be the one afraid to let someone down and would avoid saying anything at all. This likely communicates to that person that you do not care enough to tell them, even though that may not be the case.

The reason I am using this scenario is because I think it can tie into understanding communication in marriage. It is easy to communicate something in an unintended way, either verbally or by saying nothing at all. It is also easy to assume your spouse's words, actions, or lack thereof mean something completely different than they actually do mean.

For me to avoid making someone feel a certain way that I am not intending, I explain myself in every situation and detail. I do this because, while I have the ability to understand and not get upset, others may not, which can lead to them overthinking or feeling/understanding it as lack of caring. When you are self-aware of your feelings and reasoning behind why you act a certain way, it helps you to verbally explain that to your spouse so they are likely to respond in a positive way rather than a negative or angry way. There are multiple similar examples of this I can use to explain this in marriage.

For me, I am slow to anger. However, sometimes this is because I let stress build up inside and hide it, which is a flaw I am always working on with the Lord's help. My anger is mild as it comes out in the form of getting upset or crying over something stupid. The saying "don't cry over spilled milk" is literal for me. Once the stress is built up enough, I will literally cry over spilled milk. Is the reason I am upset because of the milk?—not at all. I will explain and communicate to my husband the reason behind my emotions, which is likely something along the lines of "I am so sorry I have had the most stressful week at work. I am probably hormonal, and I feel overwhelmed with everything I need to get done around the house." He is understanding, never gets mad at me for being upset, and is my voice of reason and calms me. It is the same way when the roles are reversed. We learned from each other how to know why we are feeling the way we do, why we react the way we do, and how to communicate that to each other so we can understand each other. This not only helps avoid conflict, it brings a more intimate form of communication with your spouse.

The next example important to discuss is silent communication, meaning nothing is communicated verbally but is communicated via body language. I will dig deeper into body language later in the chapter. You likely know and can read your spouse's body language and facial expression very well; after all, you are married. The problem is, how easy it is to misinterpret the well-known body language and facial expressions under certain circumstances. Large amounts of stress are something that everyone deals with, yet each person deals with it differently. The most common stress side effect for both me and my husband is always thinking about the stress. This leads to lack of focus due to the thoughts about the stress being louder than being able to hear someone talk to you. To elaborate, if you have ever been daydreaming, and someone is calling your name or talking to you, you do not hear a word they are saying, and you usually must be snapped out of it. I tend to be an overthinker, especially during a hardship in life, and I thank God for giving me the strength every time to overcome that. When it does happen, I usually have my resting face I discussed earlier that looks upset or mean. My husband will ask me, "Are you mad at me?" My body language starts to make him overthink, as if he did something wrong when he didn't. The takeaway is that he asks me if something is wrong or if I am upset instead of assuming. I then explain what I am stressed about or thinking about. Never assume your spouse's body language means what you think. Always ask what they are communicating. If you are the one communicating what your body language means, be honest with the reason, even if it is something your spouse did that is bothering you.

If you have ever read any books about learning body language or how criminal interrogators read body language, you will learn that the human body reacts in specific ways to lying. It is easy to pick up these signs in others when you learn them. Your heart may beat faster, you may sweat or get clammy, your eyes avoid eye contact and look a certain direction, your voice goes up ten octaves, you tap your leg, switch postures uncomfortably, may cross your arms to feel safe or show you are hiding something, and so on.

I am the world's worst liar. I really don't have the ability to lie because it is so obvious, and I am such a guilty conscious, even throwing a surprise party for my husband makes me feel guilty. I am a "smile or nervous laugh when I lie" type of person. If my husband asks if I am planning anything for his birthday, and I lie and say "nooooo" with my voice sounding like a ten-year-old girl, a triple chin 'cause I am looking down and pulling my face in closer to my chest. I am like Brick from the show *The Middle* when he whispers to himself, "I'm lying." The fear of lying is the best way to prevent lying in my or Brick's case.

You may have been told growing up to "always tell the truth because it is harder to remember a lie." We learn from a young age not to lie, not only does the lie hurt others, but it plants a seed within us that starts to sprout and produce guilt, shame, and love to grow colder. If your parents were anything like my parents, they just wanted the truth, even if it felt like the end of the world to you. I learned at a young age. I lied about it so much to my parents because I was terrified of getting in trouble or letting them down. We all have lied. And if you say you have not, you are lying now (insert laugh). I liked to blame my younger brothers for everything that I did. When we are kids, we are still learning what is right and what is wrong. In fact, our whole lives, we are constantly learning, and we learn most through communication.

In marriage, it is easy to quickly learn that lying to your spouse sets you back and breaks trust easily, no matter how small the lie is. While the truth is uncomfortable sometimes, it is imperative to communicate the truth in love, whether it is something that is an issue in the marriage, something you did, how you feel about a situation or a person, and so on. When you are on the receiving end of your spouse, telling you the truth about something, it is also vital to be understanding, put yourselves in their shoes the best you can, have empathy, and respect the fact they are telling you the truth. Trust can be built stronger from this. And again, I will emphasize how quickly trust can be broken. When you are actively always seeking to be honest with your spouse, no matter how big or small, they are likely to respond by always being honest with you, which leads to a worry-free marriage when it comes to trust.

Do not be afraid to communicate anything to your spouse. Your spouse likely appreciates the communication. And when you don't communicate when it is needed, it can lead to regret or conflict.

The reason I can know what my husband needs is because I have learned his way of communication and asked the Lord to help me understand what he needs or how he is feeling. While reading books, like this one, is great, the way we tend to learn best as humans is through our own experience and counting on the Lord to provide wisdom and discernment, especially with communication.

CHAPTER 5

Making Decisions Together

This chapter is going to bring together everything we have discussed already, as making decisions together depends on knowing your spouse, growing together, having quality time to make decisions together, and being able to communicate when making decisions together. When you are married, you are a team working together to make both big and small decisions together.

While communication is one of the biggest relationship killers, finances are also another big relationship killers. My opinion on why this the case is because financial decisions are not made together, or there is a disagreement about the way money is handled and spent.

What may work for one marriage may not work for another when it comes to finances. I have heard couples who keep their money together and share it in an account has worked best for them. Keeping money separate also works for others. In our case, we have kept our money separate since the beginning, and it has worked well for us. We don't keep money from each other. We always help each other and communicate about our bills and money willingly and joyfully.

Since finances are such a big part of marriage, one of the most important decisions you can make is figuring out who is best with finances and letting them voice what is best for your situation. Learning to manage finances and self-discipline when it comes to spending money is hard to do but important in order to avoid disagreements about money. This can take a lot of trial and error, so be patient.

My husband and I have had to learn a lot about managing money in a lot of the unprecedented times in which we are all living in right now, especially with inflation. Include the Lord in all of your decisions but especially financial decisions, and ask Him for what you need. Times can get tough, but the Lord will always provide right when you need it because His timing is perfect, and He has never once failed us.

I want to provide further insight into how keeping our money separate has worked for us. Some may question the reasoning as to why we keep our money separate. The main reason is how it started and worked for us from the beginning. We have always helped each other out, even before we were married. When I first met my husband—I think we were together for only maybe a month—I had just filed bankruptcy. I needed new tires on my vehicle, and he bought me tires, trusting me to pay him back. Of course I did pay him back. That built our financial trust very early on. I thought he was a crazy person at first for trusting someone so much he barely knew, but we already had built that trust with each other in a short amount of time, which is hard to do. From then on, if he needed any help, I helped him, and he always helped me. There has never been a time once in our relationship or marriage that we have not helped the other one out.

The biggest concern we have had about sharing money does not come from each other but from what we have witnessed in other marriages. We have seen disagreements over how money is spent, why it was spent, or why there is not enough money, and that has deterred us enough to keep it separate to avoid risking that situation. Another reason is because we both work full-time. We both earn our own money, so we like to have that as our own. This is not in a selfish way as we do communicate about finances; it is just more of a peace it brings to us both since we have already had a system down that works for us. Since he makes more than I do, he willingly takes responsibility for most of the bills, and he lets me focus on paying my own bills, some of our shared bills, and we use my extra income to save for vacations or to be able to have date nights. While this works for us, it may not work for everyone, so it is important to figure out what works best for your marriage and stick with that system.

The point I want to emphasize when it comes to making financial decisions together is, no matter how you keep your money (together or separate), make sure you are communicating always about your finances and stay on the same page with spending. Sometimes sacrifices must happen, and you must give up something you want to have or do because bills are the most important. Make sure your bills are paid first always, but also make sure you do put money aside sometimes for fun or date nights. Life is a balance of work and fun. Hard work is rewarding; however, marriage needs that balance so that it is not just work all the time but the ability to have fun and spend time with your spouse. If your spouse says, "No, we cannot afford this," agree with them. It takes a lot of sacrifice and understanding when it comes to finances in marriage in order for the marriage to succeed and not fail because of financial disagreement.

My husband and I meet in the middle with our views of money. He has the "you can't take it with you when you go" mentality, and I have the "let's get this paid off before we make any bigger financial decisions" mentality. He is freer with spending, I am more strict. However, we now view money at the halfway point of those points. I am able to become less strict, and he is able to become a little less free, so our decisions are balanced and in agreement with each other. Communication is a deciding factor in what your financial future will look like because communication about financial decisions has to always be present. This is especially important when it comes to making big financial decisions. There should always be a conversation and agreement between the both of you, and include God in it too! Pray for it. And if you both feel peace about it and agree, make the decision to make that purchase. If one or both of you do not feel at peace about it, listen to the lack of peace and wait. Overall, the decisions should be made together with both of you feeling at peace with any financial decision.

While financial decisions tend to be the biggest decisions made together in a marriage, there are many decisions that are made together in marriage, both big and small. When you got married, you became one flesh, therefore making decisions together in agreement, no matter how small it may seem, is vital for your marriage. Decisions can require sacrifice from one or both of you. If your spouse's reasoning makes sense, even if you are wanting a different decision, it usually means their decision is likely the best decision, and it is safe to agree with them. I will provide some examples to explain this point.

The first example I want to discuss relates to listening to the feeling in both your spirit and your spouse's spirit. One time, my husband and I bought concert tickets, and we were really excited to go. When it was time to go, I felt in my spirit that we should not go. I had no idea why; I just had a very uneasy and unsettling feeling. I explained it to my husband, and he was disappointed of course. I was disappointed as well, as we both were excited to go. However, he trusted that feeling in my spirit from the Lord, and we stayed. I found out later that not only were there multiple highway accidents on the highway between our home and where we were going, but there were also multiple shootings near exactly where we were going to go. Would this have impacted us if we went? We don't know for sure, but I know that there was something the Lord was protecting us from that day and a reason we did not go. We did not question it, and we were not upset with each other. We made that decision together, and we did not regret it.

There have been multiple times where we have listened to the others feeling in the spirit, and it may disappoint sometimes, but there is always a good reason behind it. We have also learned the hard way of not listening to that feeling in our spirit. There was another time we went out of town to visit my brother, and he offered to let us stay the night. I told my husband I think we should stay, but he wanted to drive home. I listened to him, and we went; however, we came upon a terrible snowstorm, and he could not see the road at all when he was driving. It was not visible conditions and was scary, especially on the highway. Luckily, the Lord protected us, and we were able to get off at the next exit and get a hotel for the night.

This is an extreme example, but we both have had our fair share of not listening to the other and learning the hard way. Sometimes we, as humans, need to learn the hard way so we can take that knowledge and apply it to future decisions we make, and that is okay! God speaks to us through each other a lot so that is why listening to each other and making those decisions together can change a whole scenario or avoid a bad situation.

The next example relates to making decisions out of love. It is popular in the world today to live for yourself and do whatever you want to do. This lifestyle should be nonexistent in your marriage. This is not to say that you don't get to ever do anything you want; however, in marriage, after Jesus, your spouse comes first. There is nothing more important to me in this world than my husband. He comes first no matter what. When it comes to making decisions out of love, sometimes we both have to make the sacrifice and not get to do what we want. My husband and I have learned this over time, and it is not always easy to learn. If there is something I really want to do, my husband will usually always do it, even if he is not that interested in doing it, and I will do the same for him. However, there are times when one of us feels we want to do something, but the other really does not feel up to it. It is important to distinguish the difference between not wanting to do something and not feeling up to it. If your spouse is telling you they are not feeling up to it because they are not feeling well or are feeling drained, it is important to listen to that and respect that. Instead of getting disappointed, I just say, "It's okay. I understand because I know that feeling. and you are more important than what I want to do." We know when to make those decisions out of love. whether it is to sacrifice and do something we do not like necessarily or to sacrifice not doing something we want to do for the sake of our spouse's needs.

My husband and I, even before we were married, were always making decisions together. Communication plays a big factor when it comes to making decisions. We have always communicated to each other when making any decision, even something as small as what we are eating for dinner. When you make decisions together, you are showing each other that you are playing on the same team, and it shows one another how committed you are to each other's feelings and opinions. Continue to make decisions together throughout your marriage, and you will see the positive results and rewards for doing so.

CHAPTER 6

Marriage Truths and Marriage Misconceptions

In this chapter, I want to cover how a successful, happy, and healthy marriage has already been laid out for us, as well as the common misconceptions about marriage. By now you have learned that marriage is about serving your spouse, just as we serve the Lord and your marriage is to reflect the love for each other that Christ has for us. People misrepresent the faith and God, which would make them not actually of the faith or of God, and you have to be able to separate the truth from human behavior. This goes for marriage as well. Seeing marriage represented in a way that is not good does not mean that marriage is not good. The human behavior in that specific bad marriage does not speak for actual marriage, just like a misrepresentation of God through specific human behavior does not speak for the truth of the faith. Just like society cannot run in a stable fashion based on feelings and emotions, neither can marriage. Marriage has to have truth and objectives to stand on to keep you grounded so you are not making decisions or saying things based on emotions like the world teaches you to do. Marriage cannot be subjective, so you cannot have a stable marriage if it is only based on how you feel.

In order to understand the misconceptions of marriage, I think it is important to understand the objective truths about marriage first that were outlined for us thousands of years ago in the number one bestselling book of all time, which is the written word of God: the Bible! I want to share verses about marriage, explain the meaning, and how you can apply the aliveness of the Word to your own marriage, just as we have.

When you get married, it is a serious commitment. It is not just a gathering of your loved ones and a party afterward. The vows you make are not just words you say; the vows are alive and meant to be lived out until death does you part. The world has watered down the seriousness of marriage, which is heartbreaking to witness. However, those who do take it seriously find a very blessed gift from God and see the blessing in the marriage. We all want God to bless us, and He certainly does bless marriages that live out their vows and listen to His words that are alive and show us how to live in our marriages. My husband and I are living proof of the blessing and the multitude of fruits produced in our marriage and in our lives together.

In Matthew 7:13–14, Jesus said, "Enter by the narrow gate. For the gate is wide and the way is easy that leads to destruction, and those who enter it are many. For the gate is narrow, and the way is hard that leads to life, and those who find it are few." This parable is specifically talking about the path we take in life that leads to life or death. Jesus is telling His disciples to take the narrow path, which is the opposite of the path of the world. The narrow path is hard. Jesus never promised us that life would be easy following Him; He just promised that following Him leads to life and that He is with us through all of our hardships. If we apply this verse to our marriage, it is similar because it is easy to just go from relationship to relationship, leave when things get hard, and live life the way we want or view marriage as a hard burden, like the world seems to do. Marriage is not easy, just like the narrow path is not easy, but marriage is worth the hard work and full of blessings when you have the right mindset and heart. This is also required while taking the hard path of following Jesus and going against the world's path.

When God commands us to do anything, it is not because He is being mean; He is giving you the guidance to do what is in your best interest and for His glory. God sees and hears things you cannot see or hear so you can trust Him to lead and guide your marriage, just as you trust Him to guide and lead your life. I want to now discuss the commands God gives us for love and marriage.

First Corinthians 16:14 says, "Do everything in love." This means to literally do everything in love. This is applied not just to marriage but to everyone. Think about how much Jesus loved you, even before you were saved or knew how much He loved you. When you look back now, you realize how much love He had for you, even when you were far from Him and rejecting Him. God never stopped loving you, even when you did not love Him. There is no greater love than this, and this is the kind of love that is meant to be in your marriage, to mirror the love God has for you to your spouse. John 15:12 reads, "My command is this: love each other as I have loved you." The unconditional love God has for us is the unconditional love you are to have for your spouse.

Ephesians 4:52 says, "Be kind and compassionate to one another, forgiving each other, just as Christ forgave you." We all need kindness, compassion, and forgiveness. Romans 3:23–24 says, "For all have sinned and fallen short of the glory of God, and are justified by the grace as a gift (a free gift), through the redemption that is in Christ Jesus." Just as Jesus forgave us, we must forgive our spouse. God sees us as sinless because of our salvation through Jesus. Just as we are forgiven, we must forgive our spouse and keep no record of wrong, as commanded in 1 Corinthians 13.

First Peter 4:8 says, "Above all, love each other deeply, because love covers a multitude of sins." When you choose to love and serve each other in your marriage, that love and servitude avoids indifference, anger, jealousy, bitterness, unfaithfulness, and so much more. Psalm 85:10 says, "Love (mercy) and faithfulness meet together; righteousness and peace kiss each other." God is always faithful to everyone who trusts in and loves Him. God's character is righteous, and His promises are always kept. When your marriage mirrors God's character and your relationship with Him, peace, love, and righteousness flow easily into your marriage.

Husbands and wives are equal in marriage and in the relationship with Jesus; however, the Scripture provides different roles for husbands and wives. Proverbs 18:22 reads, "He who finds a wife, finds what is good, and receives favor from the Lord." The Lord is pleased when a man is wise enough to make a woman his wife, and she is a blessing from the Lord to be treasured and cherished. When this takes place, husband and wife experience the oneness that God designed for them to have. I have heard multiple pastors say they have read the Bible front to back, and there is not one verse that says this about husbands (to make it humorous). Husbands, finding and keeping a wife really is a good thing.

One of the main roles of a husband in the marriage is to be the leader of the home. This can be found in 1 Corinthians 11:3, "But I want you to understand the head of every man is Christ, the head of a wife is her husband, and the head of Christ is God" and, in Ephesians 5:23–33, "For the husband is the head of the wife, even as Christ is the head of the Church, his body, and himself its Savior." A husband as the leader is not a dictator over his wife, condescending toward his wife, and does not patronize his wife. A husband's leadership should reflect Jesus, leading as the head of the church. Ephesians 5:25–33 reads, "Husbands, love your wives, as Christ loved the church and gave himself up for her, that he might sanctify her, having cleansed her by the washing of water with the word, so that he might present the church to himself in splendor, without spot or wrinkle or any such thing, that she might be holy and without blemish. In the same way, husbands should love their wives as their own bodies. He who loves his wife loves himself (because you are one). For no one ever hated his own flesh, but nourishes it and cherishes it, just as Christ does the church, because we are members of his body. Therefore, a man shall leave his father and mother and hold fast to his wife, and the two shall be one flesh. The mystery is profound, and I am saying it refers to Christ and the church. However, let each of you love his wife as himself, and let the wife see that she respects her husband." Husbands, when you love your wife as you love yourself and respect her and her opinions/views, your wife will respect you. Colossians 3:18–19 reads, "Wives, submit to your husbands, as is fitting in the Lord. Husbands, love your wives, and do not be harsh with them." When the Lord is telling wives to submit, He is not saying it in the context of the world's definition of submission in a degrading way. Men tend to need and require respect and honor, while women tend to need love and appreciation. Wives, when you submit to your husbands, you are showing respect to your husband, valuing what they have to say and their opinions, and showing your husband they are important, honored, valued, and trusted in their leadership role. This does not mean you are to follow and listen to everything they say without an opinion or say (like the world tends to view submission), but when there is mutual respect in your marriage, you both are able to submit to one another in a healthy, Christlike way. When love and respect meet and come together, a healthy and happy marriage results and thrives.

Another one of the primary roles of husbands is to be the provider of the household. My husband is such a blessing and works so hard to provide for us and takes great joy in doing so. In the times we are living in, it is hard to live on one income, and it is okay and perfectly normal for wives to work and bring in income too. I love to work and help provide. I have always been independent and always found a way to provide for myself and others, as it brings me joy to do so. When I met my husband, I surrendered to the extreme independence I had and allowed myself to accept and allow my husband to be the primary provider. Before I met him, I was so used to being the one that provided and in survival mode, but I was able to lay that down because I saw how important it was to my husband to provide for me as it is an important to most husbands. (It should be to all, especially those who follow Jesus.) A wife's primary role is to take care of the house and the kids. However, just like providing can be both, taking care of the house and kids should be both as well. I personally, as a wife, take great pride in helping keep up around the house (especially the kitchen. That is my favorite place to be). I love to cook; it brings me such peace, joy, and teaches me a lot.

If you have ever heard of a Proverbs 31 woman, that is the woman I have strived to be and continue to strive to be in my marriage for my husband. The Proverbs 31 woman is described in Proverbs 31:10–31. Verses 10 through 12 reads, "An excellent wife who can find? She is far more precious than jewels. The heart of her husband trusts in her, and he will have no lack of gain. She does him good, and not harm, all of the days of her life." My favorite is verses 25 through 31, which reads, "Strength and dignity are her clothing, and she laughs at the time to come. She opens her mouth with wisdom, and the teaching of kindness is on her tongue. She looks well to the ways of her household and does not eat the bread of idleness. Her children rise up and call her blessed; her husband also, and he praises her: 'Many women have done excellently, but you surpass them all.' Charm is deceitful, and beauty is vain, but a woman who fears the Lord is to be praised. Give her the fruit of her hands, and let her works praise her in the gates." Wives, when you seek the wisdom of God and not of this world, everything comes naturally for you, especially in your marriage. In a world so focused on comparing, good looks, material items, as a Proverbs 31 woman, you are not seeking or interested in the things of this world but the riches of the wisdom and guidance of the Lord.

Proverbs 12:4 reads, "A wife of noble character is her husbands crown, but a disgraceful wife is like decay in his bones." Wives, when you are a woman of character, you are loving toward your husbands. You honor him, respect him. He will be so full of thankfulness and joy. When you shame or mistreat your husband with a heart of foolishness or selfishness, it will slowly kill him on the inside. First Peter 3:3–4, speaking to women, says, "Your beauty should not come from outward adornment, such as elaborate hairstyles and the wearing of gold jewelry or fine clothes. Rather, it should be that of your inner self, the unfading beauty of a gentle and quiet spirit, which is of great worth in God's sight." Wives, remember that God looks at the heart. And when you do have a gentle and quiet spirit, your husband will see the reflection of God's character in you, and that is what makes you truly beautiful. There will always be someone prettier, someone with better clothes, and so on, but those things are fleeting, and true beauty comes from the condition of your heart and character.

For my husband and I, when we met, we were both at a point where all we wanted was peace in life. In our almost six years of relationship, there has been peace between us for, I would say, 99 percent of the time. Earlier, I shared a verse about how finding a wife is a good thing. So wives, this is where you may feel convicted. Proverbs 25:24 reads, "Better to live on the corner of the roof than share a house with a quarrelsome wife." This means exactly what it says. It is better to live on the roof, where there is peace, than to live in a house with an argumentative/quarrelsome wife. This is draining to a husband and strips him of his peace. In order to have a happy, healthy, successful marriage, peace is vital in both husbands and wives. You should be each other's peace, just as God provides peace for you both.

As you can see, the word of God gives us a stable foundation that gives us purpose and meaning outside of what the world says. The firm foundation for marriage is found in the Word, and God teaches us how to value your husband/wife. When you both agree on the truth, you won't always be perfect, but you will be easily accountable and be able to change. Marriage is vulnerable to failure when there is not a firm foundation based on objective truth in place. Give up selfishness. The world is teaching you to be your own god and do what you want to feel good, but that mindset does not work in marriage. Marriage was designed to be an agreement together with God until death.

While there is a lot more than can be covered and much more that can be learned, I wanted to write this book to give a simple start to help and understand that healthy, happy, and successful marriages do exist. I hope my personal examples and the wisdom I have learned over the years will bless you. I do not know everything nor do I have all of the answers as I am a constant work in progress and learning each day myself. However, I hope my personal examples and the wisdom I have learned over the years will help bless you.

Seek God for truth and wisdom in your marriage, and He will answer you. Remember to journey together in your marriage to overcome your weaknesses together and laugh together often.

Quick tips and advice to always remember:

- Remember you are married to your best friend, and it is up to you both to make life fun together.
- Be each other's peace, not more added stress or pain.
- Laugh together often.

- Learn new things together (we are working on ice skating)
- Be open and vulnerable with each other. As scary as it can be or seem, it will help you grow closer and understand each other more.
- Be a safe and understanding person your spouse can trust and can talk about anything without fear of being shamed, ridiculed, or yelled at.
- Don't make your spouse feel bad or talk down to them. Lift them up with kind words and talk in a positive tone. (My husband makes fun of me in a fun way like for example how I use a pizza cutter). Fun-loving jokes toward each other keep you laughing. Just be careful not to use sarcasm/humor in a toxic way that actually insults your spouse. Also, be open to taking jokes that are harmless jokes because it makes it more fun (we make fun of each other all the time in a loving way and we love it because it keeps us laughing)
- Talk more, argue less. Always ask yourself, is this worth getting upset about?
- Don't let outside opinions affect you. They don't know your marriage like you know your marriage.
- Be careful who you go to and ask for life advice. Make sure the person you are going to is trustworthy, emotionally/spiritually mature, and wants what is best for you and your life (that is if you do go to anyone, most things are better kept between you and your spouse to discuss and work out).
- Forgive and do not hold it over your spouse's head.
- Your spouse is going to change, learn, and grow over time. It is possible to fall in love with your spouse more as they grow (I love my husband more and more each day)
- Tell your spouse how much you love them, appreciate them, and how proud you are of them. Speak words of life and love into them daily. Be their encouragement, not their discouragement (the world will do enough of that already).
- You can and will overcome anything together that life throws your way, you just both have to be willing to work

through it together, work on your own self, and focus on the lesson/growth rather than the problem.

- Focus on the good in your spouse so your mindset remains loving and positive towards them which encourages you both to grow naturally. If you are always focused on the flaws or negative, your mindset will always be negative toward them and it may discourage growth. This can cause a distance between the two of you and may cause you to lose motivation to put forth effort into the marriage yourself or lead to "checking out" of the marriage completely.

- Be patient and understanding toward each other in every situation you face together. Remember to make sure you consider what your spouse is feeling and try to understand them the best you can. Are they over-stimulated, overwhelmed, hurt, or stressed? Be gracious if they are. Are you overstimulated, overwhelmed, hurt, or stressed? Be self-aware of that and learn to control those emotions or apologize if you let the emotions get the best of you. You are both human after all!

- Your spouse cannot read your mind (although sometimes I do question if my husband can read mine). Communicate your feelings and needs and make sure they understand what you are communicating. Allow them to communicate their feelings and needs and make sure you understand what they are communicating.

- Be slow to anger and judgment. Do not assume anything.

- There is no such thing as the perfect marriage so you will have hardships. Just remember to be actively growing and learning, and allow God to help in every step and phase. One of my favorite verses to remind myself of during trials is James 1:2–5: "Count it all joy, my brothers, when you meet trials of various kinds, for you know that the testing of your faith produces steadfastness. And let steadfastness have its full effect, that you may be perfect and complete, lacking nothing. If any of you lacks wisdom, let him ask

God who gives generously to all without reproach and it will be given to him."

- We are all human and will always be flawed so have grace while you encourage one another. If you both know you do not know everything and are both open to learning as you go, you will grow and flourish together. Look at each other knowing you both are still learning so that you can teach each other, learn together, and see each other as works in progress with grace, understanding, and patience.

- Do not give your spouse a reason to question your trust. My husband has shown me what real trust is. I am safe to run to him to talk to him about anything and he is safe to run to me to talk to me about anything. He makes sure he does not put himself in a position that would make me question his trust, and I do the same thing. It is not that we do not trust each other, it is to show we care about each other enough to say, "I do not want you even to have the option to question anything because I love you and respect the trust and love we have."

- Sometimes we can be too blind to see our own faults. That is why it is important to ask your spouse what you can work on and seek God to search your heart to see what faults/weaknesses you may have. You cannot work on something or ask God to help you work on it when you are not consciously aware of it yourself. Don't feel shame for your faults, be empowered, encouraged, and strengthened to know them!

- Always consider your spouse. For example, when making even small decisions like what to eat, we consider what the other wants or likes and make an agreement together. We always discuss our plans and consider our time together to be the most important. We make sure we do not have anything planned with each other first before we make plans for anything else. We make sure to keep each other in the loop about everything and love to talk to each other about everything.

- Forgive yourselves for your past mistakes so it does not carry into your present. You learned from it and have come far from it, don't bury yourself in it. Take the time you need to unlearn the toxic effects from the past and heal. You deserve that and so does your spouse (and so do your children if you have kids)! This is hard and I struggle with it too, but it is necessary.
- Real love is rare and a gift from God. Be grateful when you have it and show others they can have it too. Make sure you never take your love/spouse for granted, appreciate it/ them now.

Quick prayer for your spouse:

Heavenly Father, I come in Jesus's name. I want to thank you for the husband/wife you have blessed me with, the roof over our heads, food to eat, water to drink, and the clothes on our bodies. Thank you for giving us the gift of discernment so we can understand each other better and grow together. Thank you for showing us grace and mercy so we are able to give each other grace and mercy every day. Thank you for forgiving us so we can forgive each other. I pray for your protection, love, and guidance over my husband/wife. I pray you give them the wisdom and strength they need to get through each day. What we don't know, please teach us so we can continue to grow and know how to love one another each day. Help me to become as patient, loving, gracious, forgiving, and understanding as you Lord.

In Jesus's name, I pray. Amen.

May God bless you, keep you, and continue to guide you both as your marriage continues to grow and flourish. I am rooting for you and praying for you!

Questions to Discuss with Your Spouse

What core values do we have in our marriage and what core values can we add or work on?

What can I work on personally to be a better spouse for you?

What is a hobby or activity you would like us to do together?

How can I communicate better?

What makes you feel loved by me? What can I do or continue to do to ensure you feel loved by me each day?

Is there any area that you feel unheard or misunderstood? If so, how can I hear and understand you better?

Danielle was born and raised in Kalamazoo, Michigan, where she resides with her husband and their nine-year-old Chihuahua-Yorkie-mix dog, Benzi. The author and her husband are a blended family and she was blessed to become a stepmom and step-grandma. Danielle loved writing from a young age and has always had a passion for helping others, so she spent her high school and college years pursuing a future career in law enforcement. She earned her degree in criminal justice at Grand Valley State University and attended the GVSU Police Academy. That career path was not the Lord's plan; however, it taught her a lot and helped shape her into who she is now. God called her to start writing in April 2023. She is passionate about helping others, spending time with friends and family, traveling, reading, writing, cooking, learning new sports, trivia, bingo, and board games. She is most passionate about her love for Jesus and allowing Him to continue to teach her and grow her each day.

* 9 7 9 8 8 8 9 2 4 3 8 7 5 9 *